Colored Pencil Drawing Inspiration Book

Pencil Drawing Refrence Book for Beginners

By Priyank Gala

Published By:

Priyank Gala

ISBN-13: 978-1508629573
ISBN-10: 1508629579

©Copyright 2015 – Priyank Gala

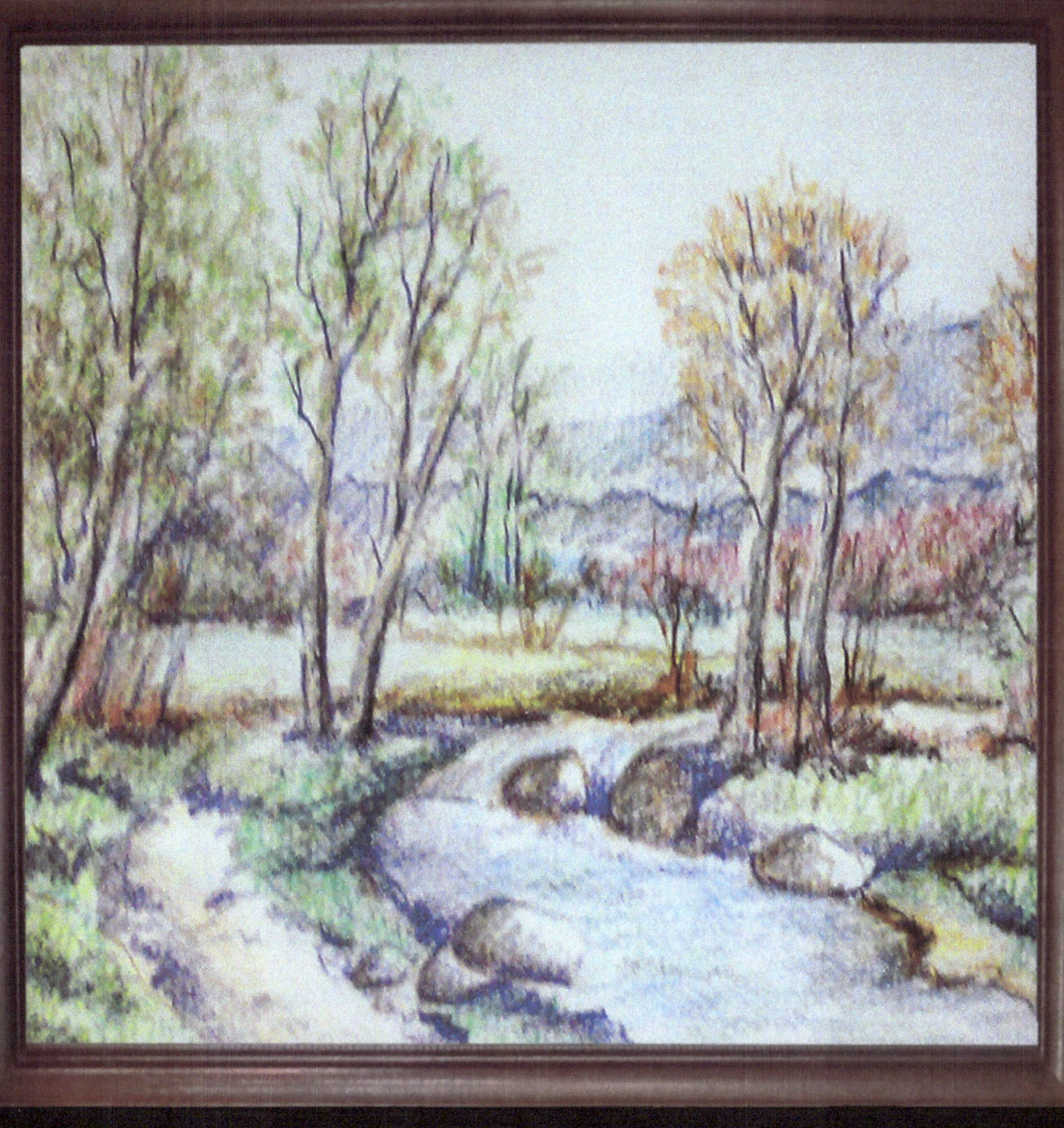

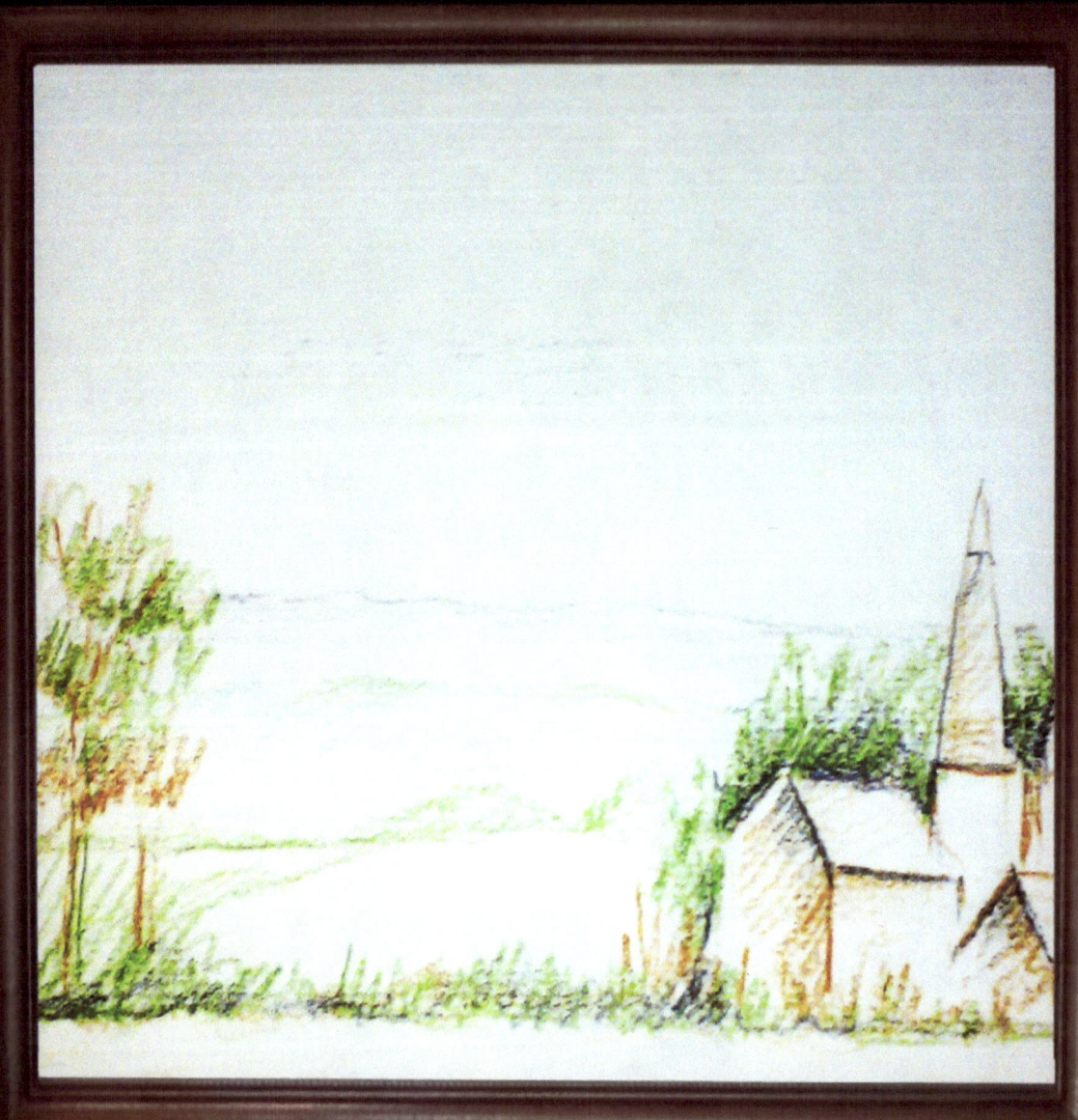

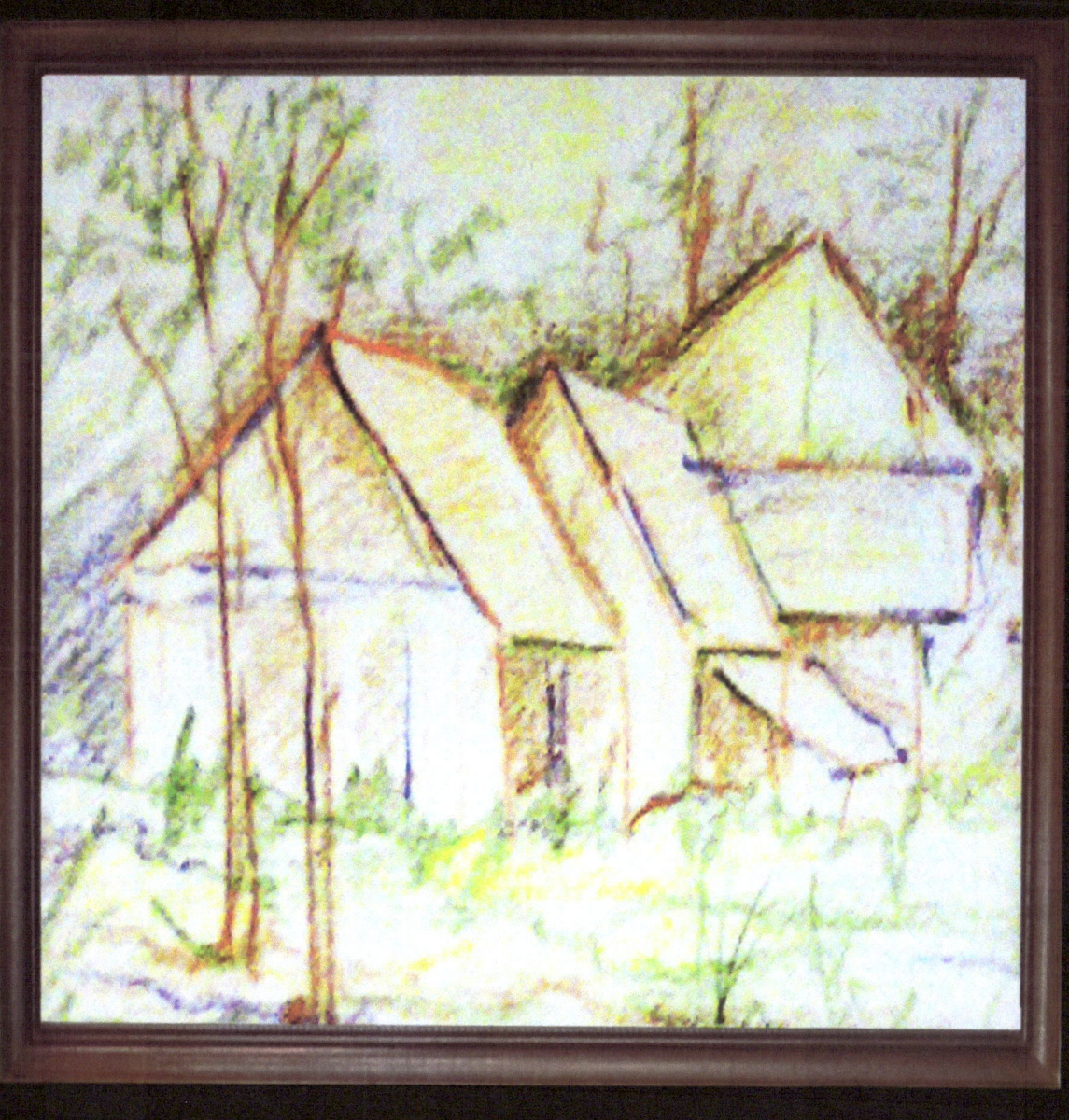

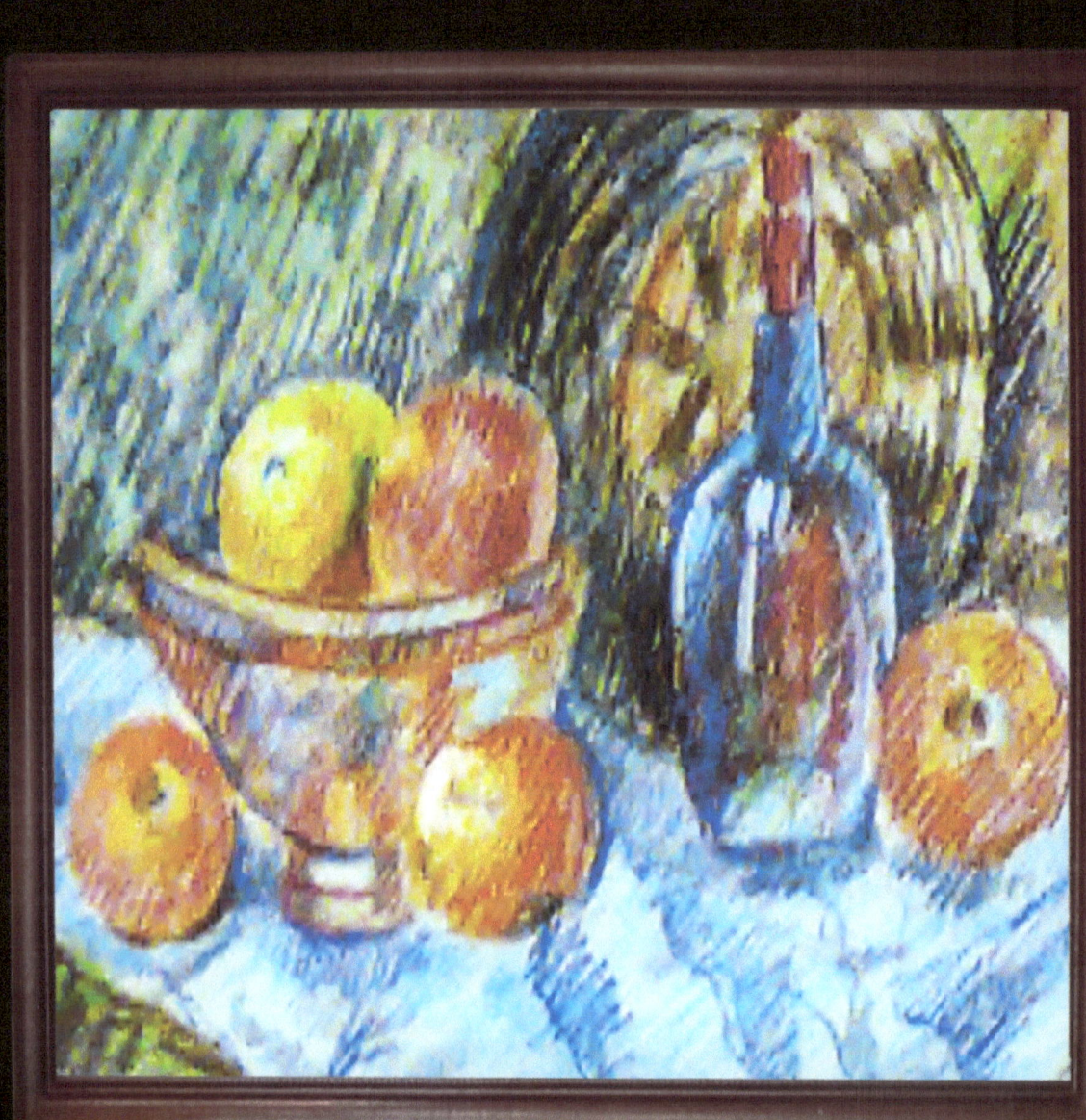

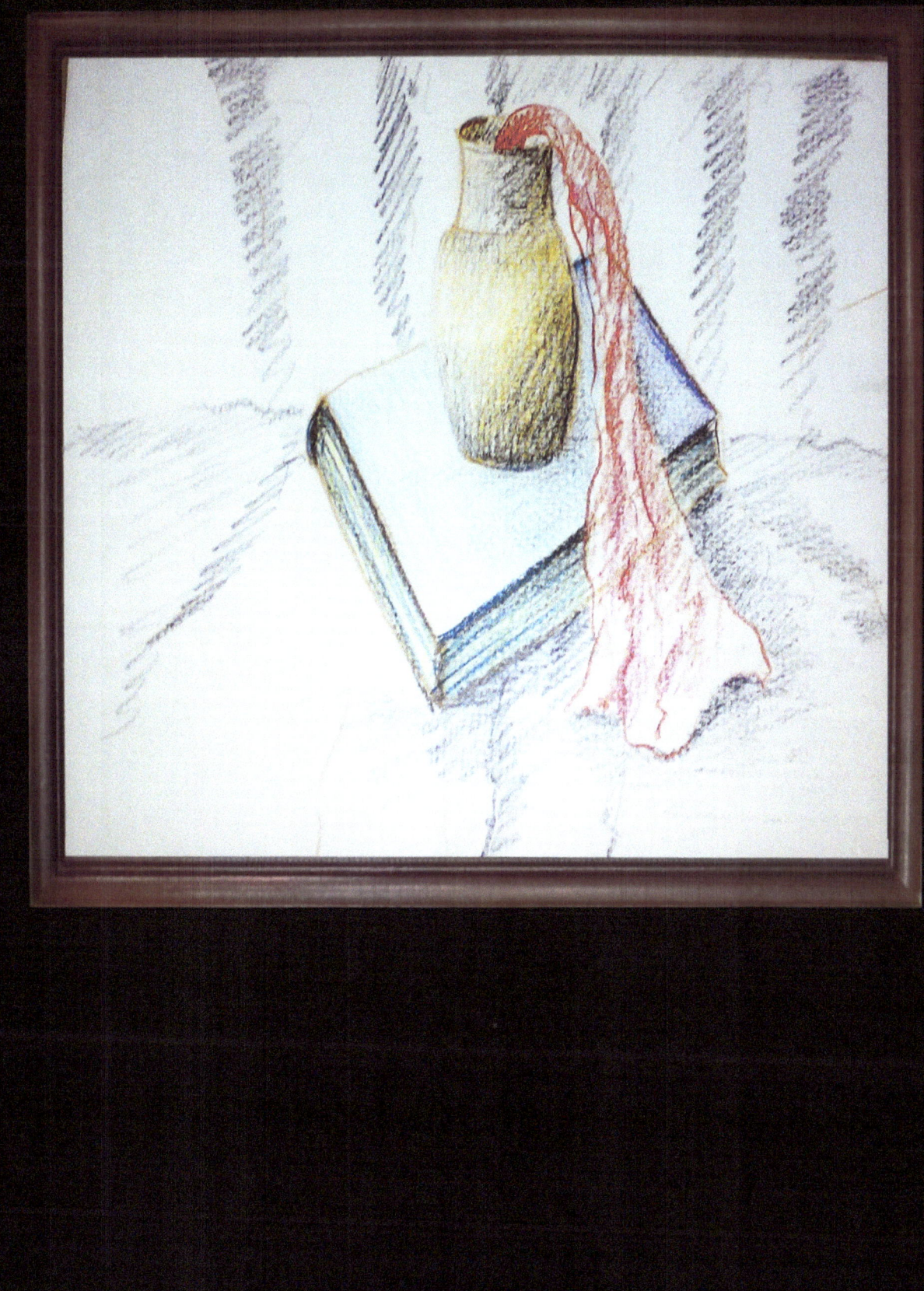

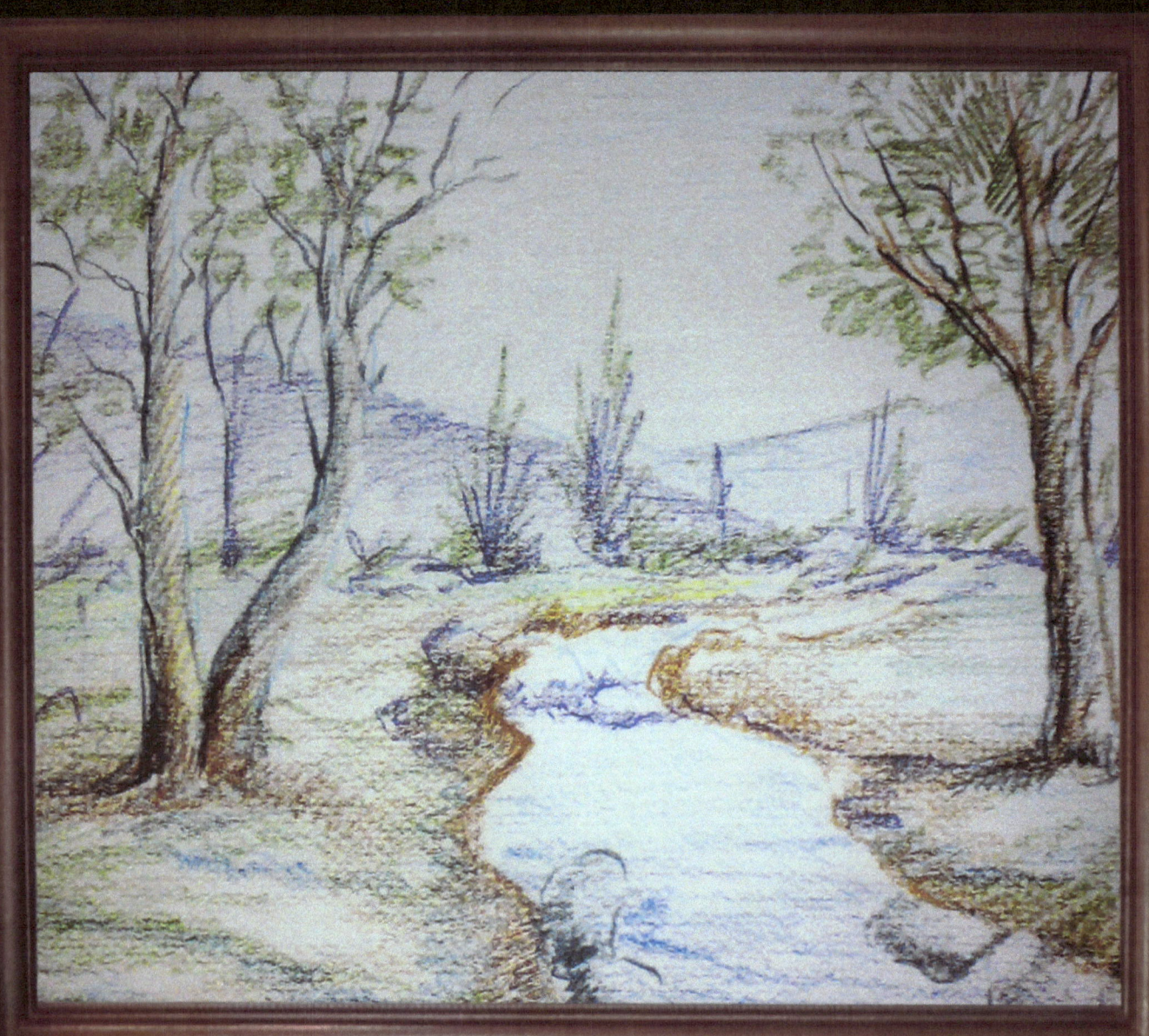

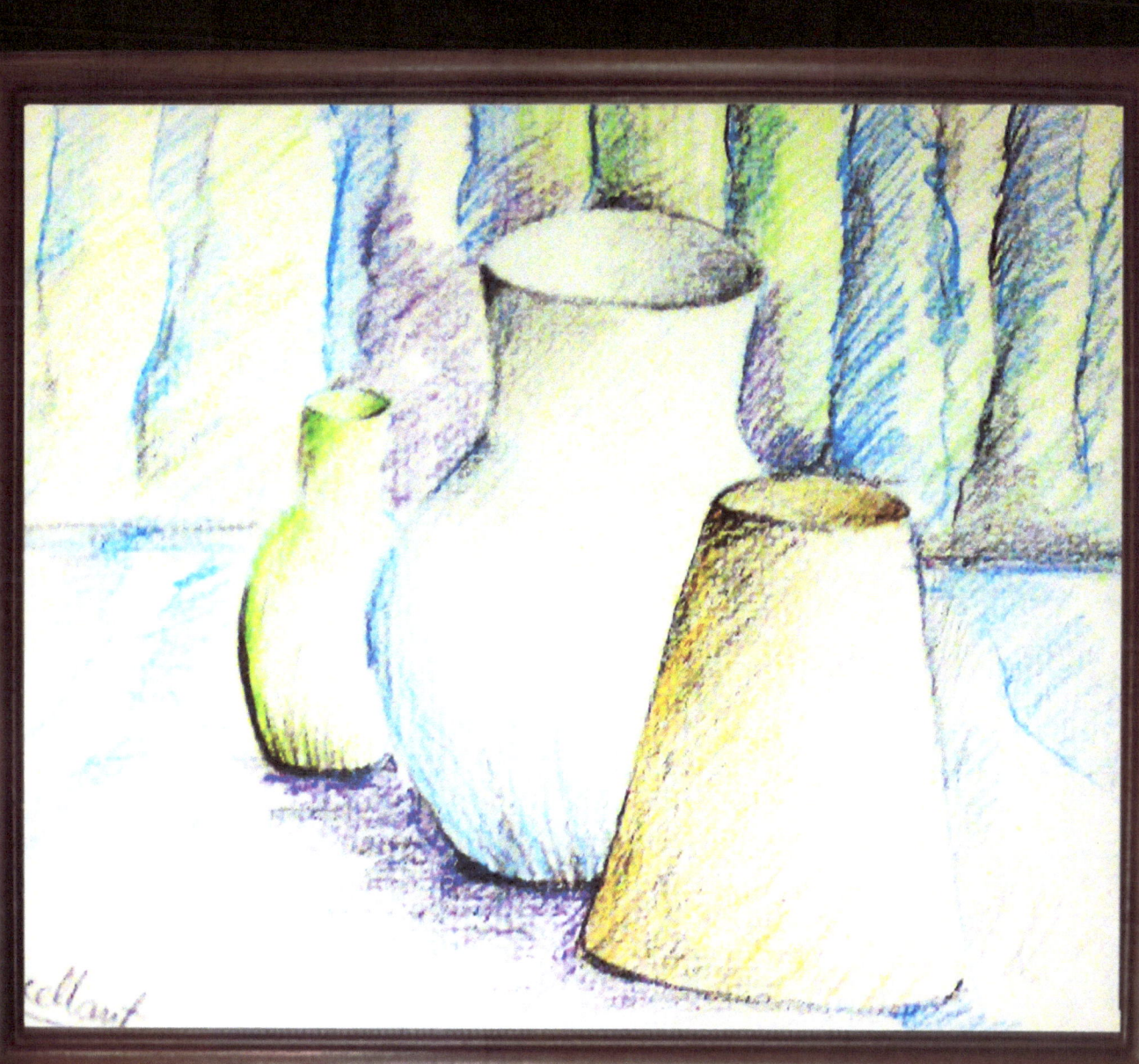

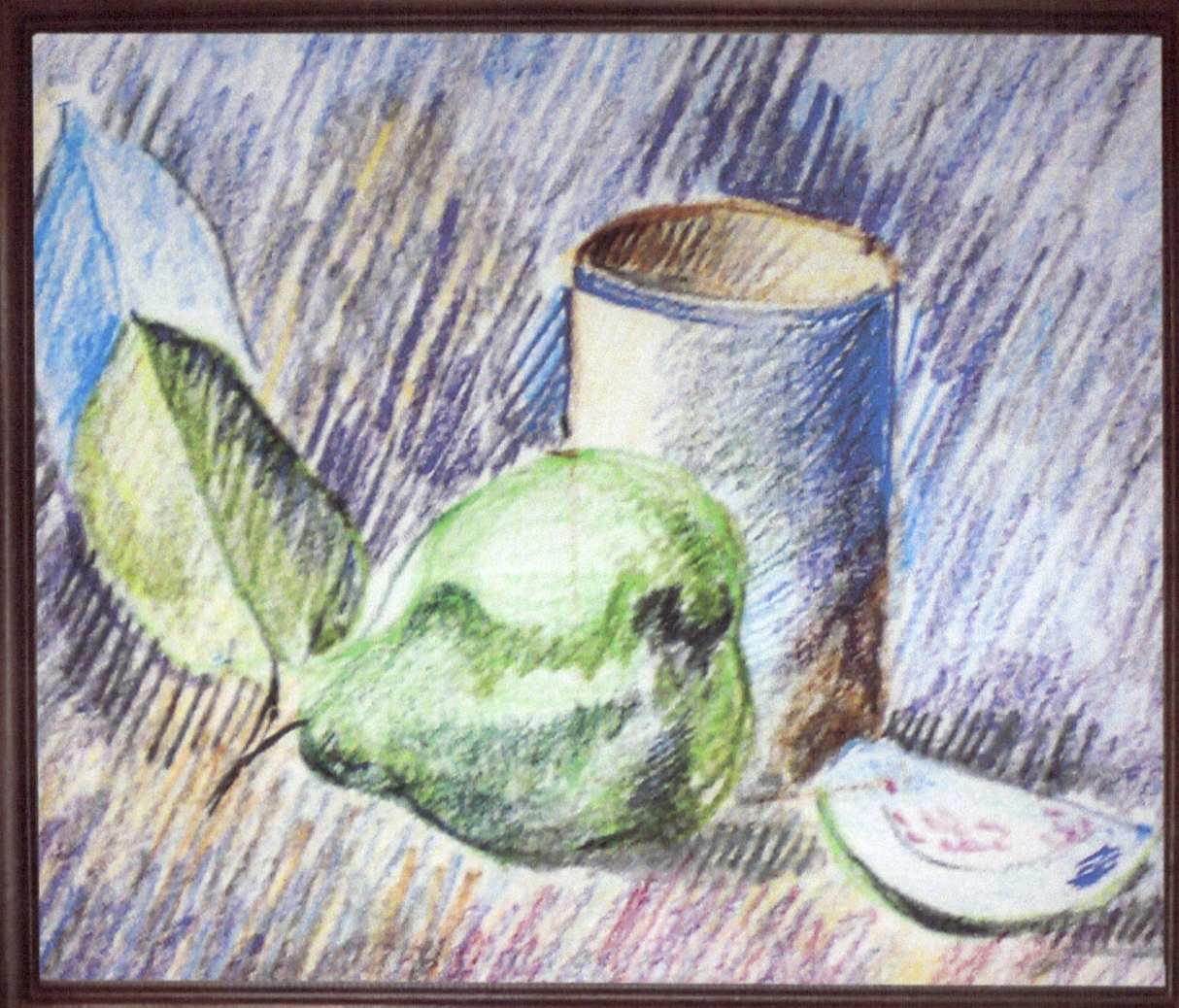

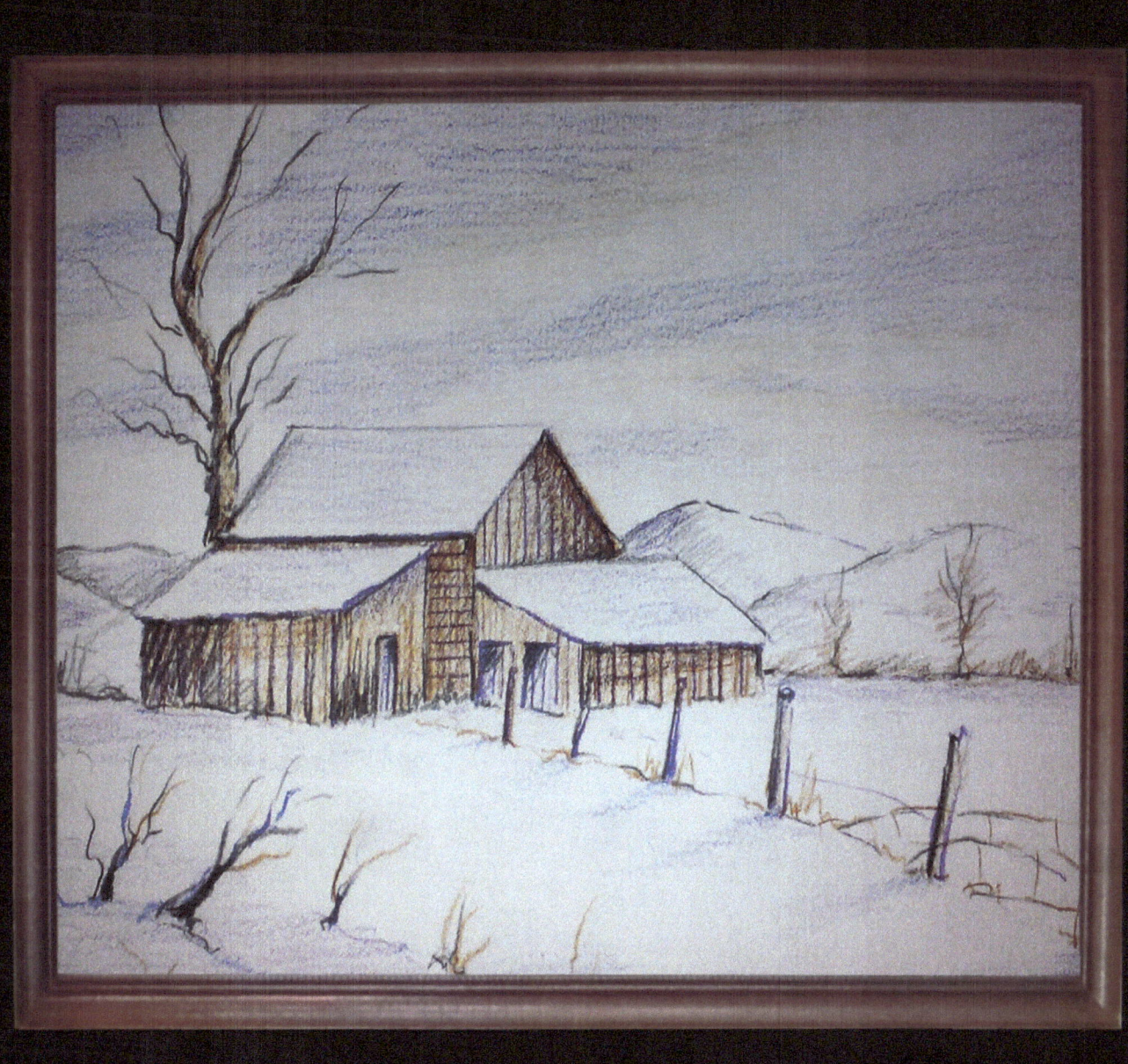

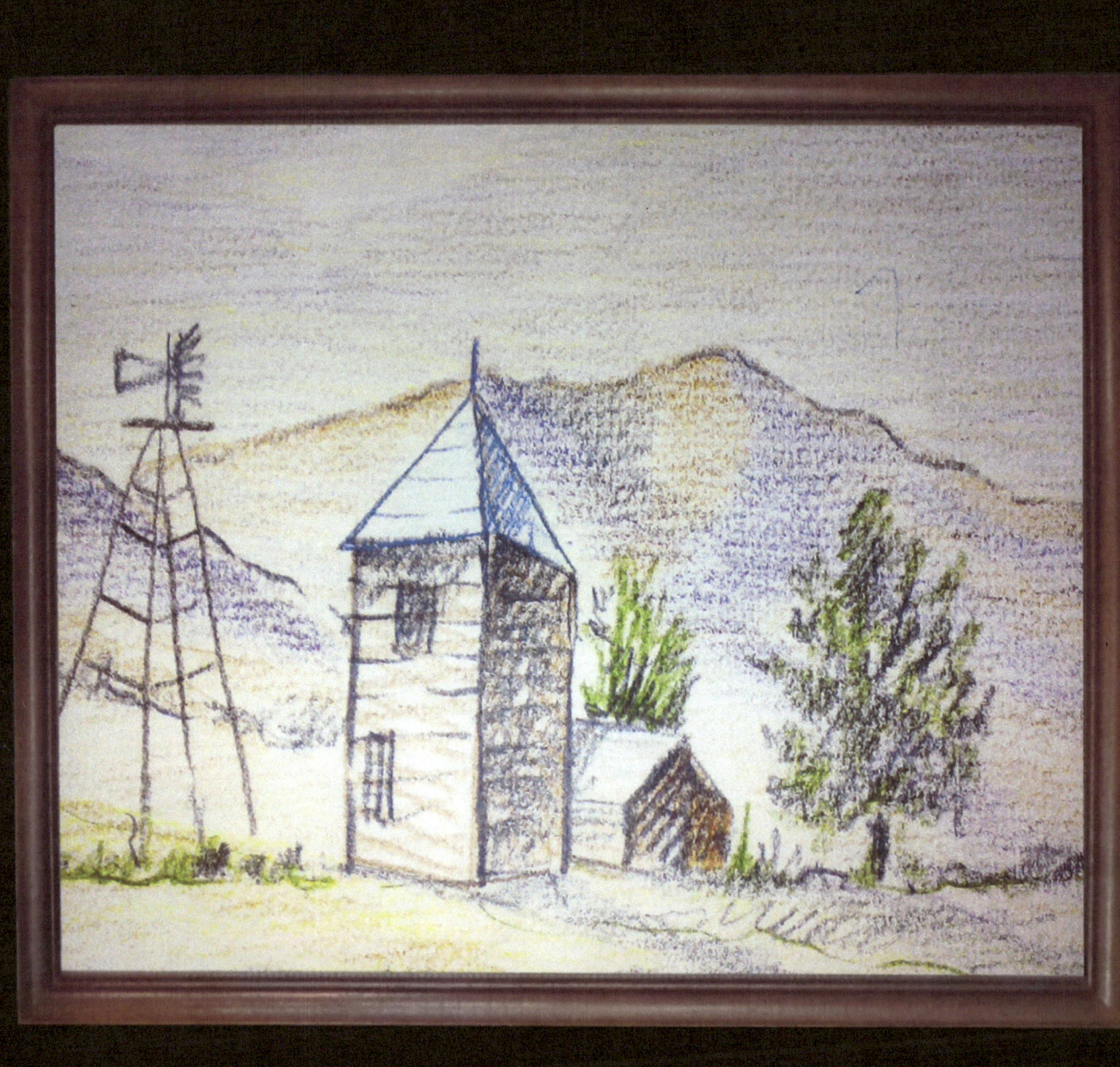

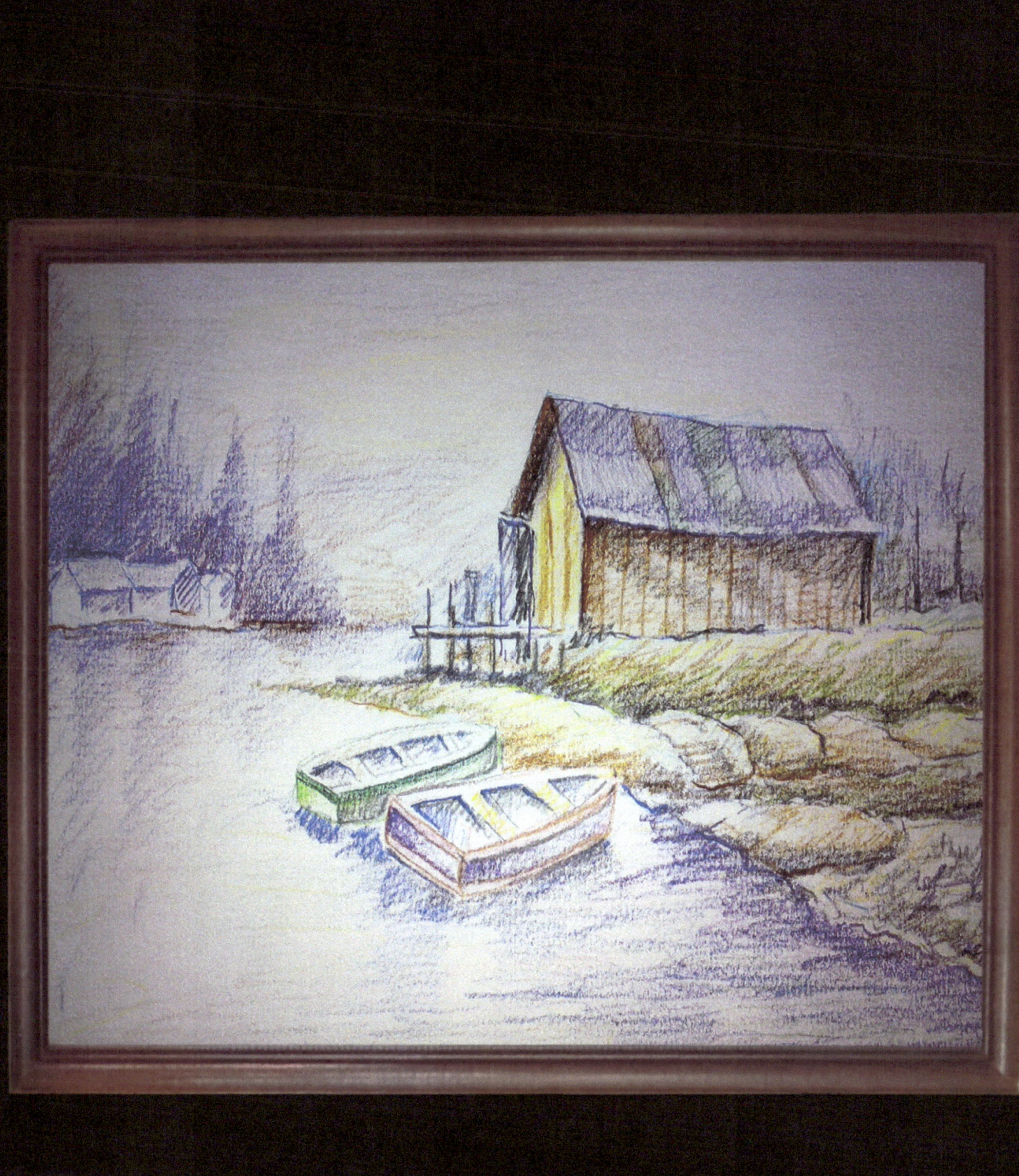

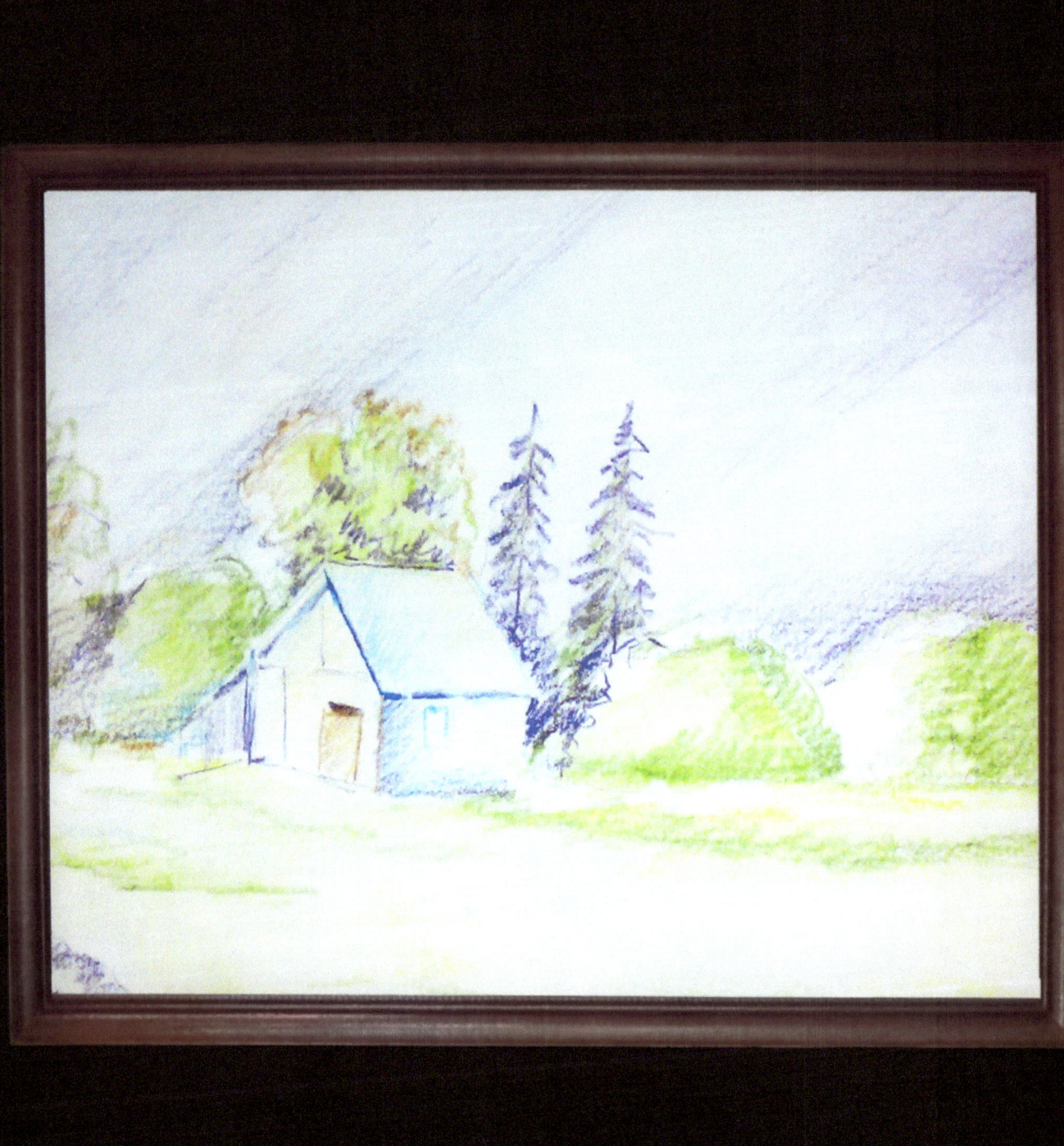

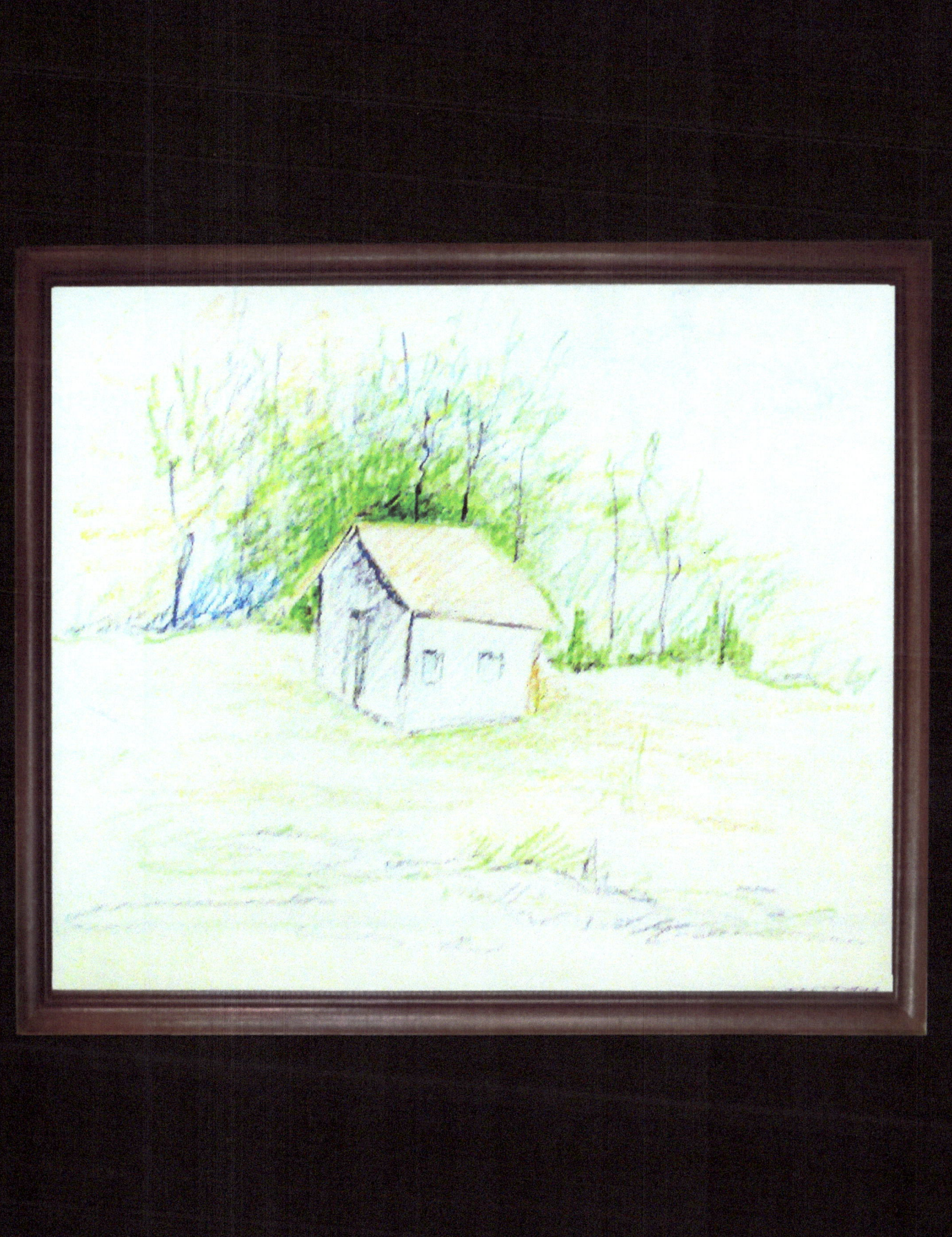

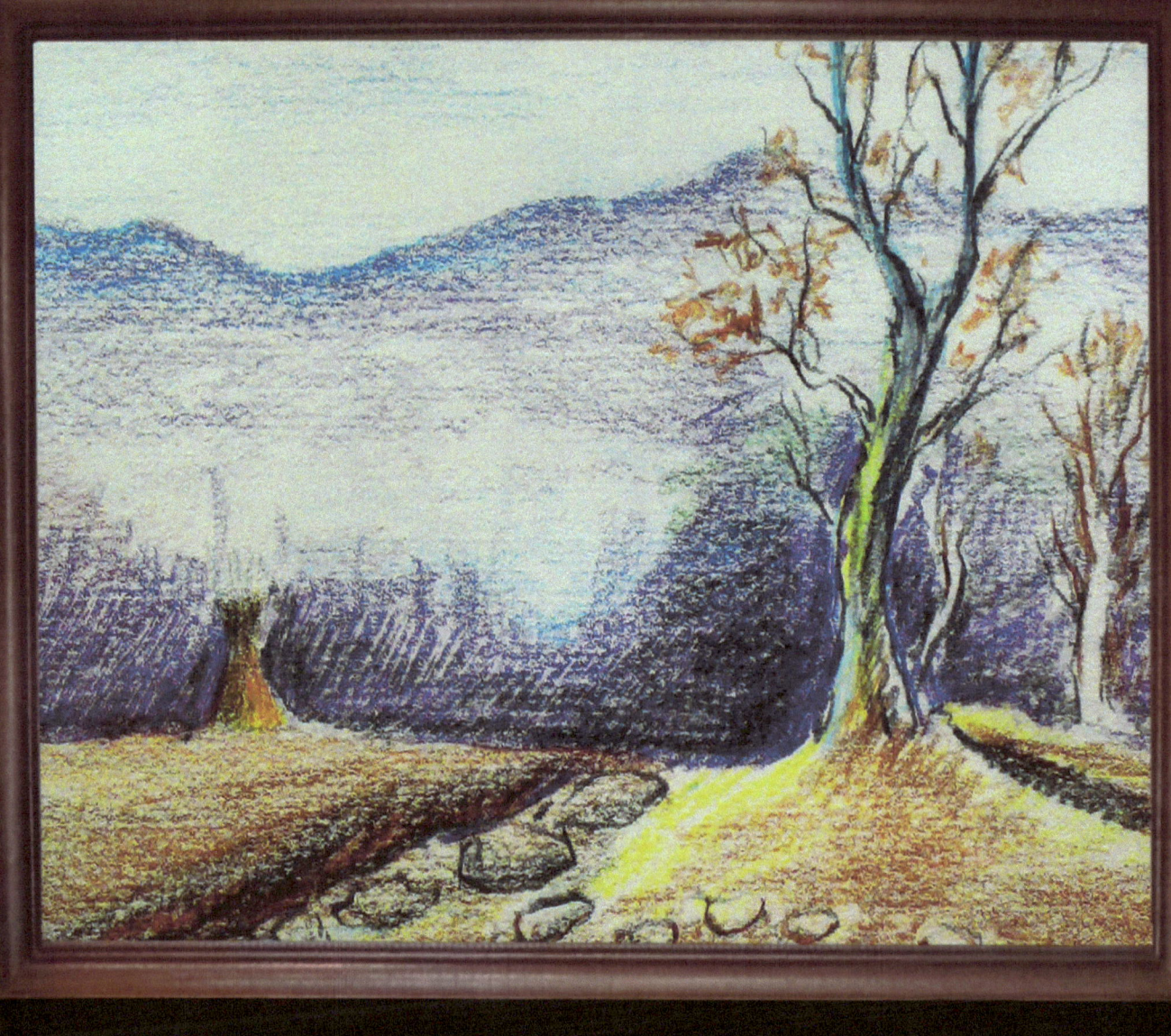

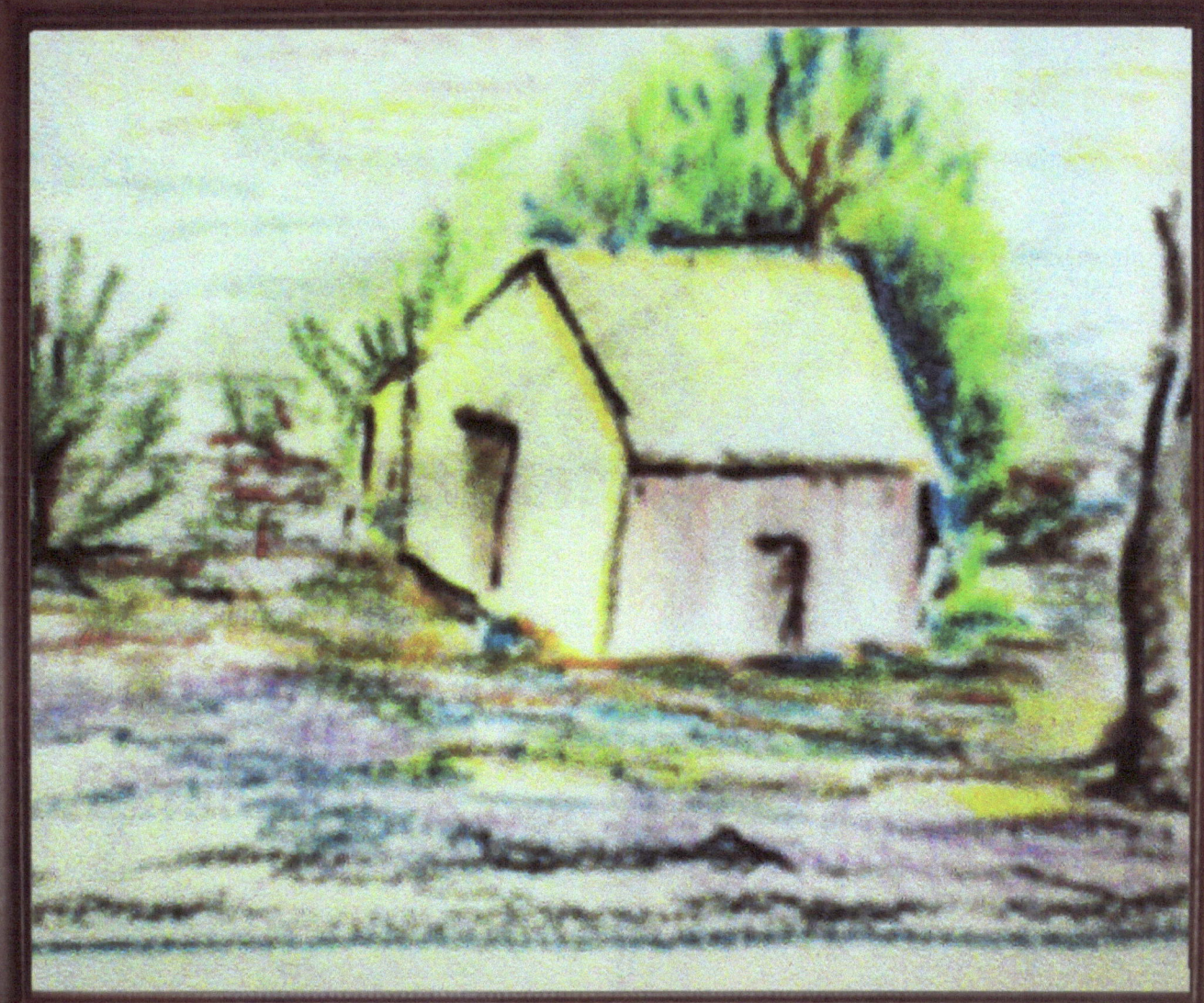

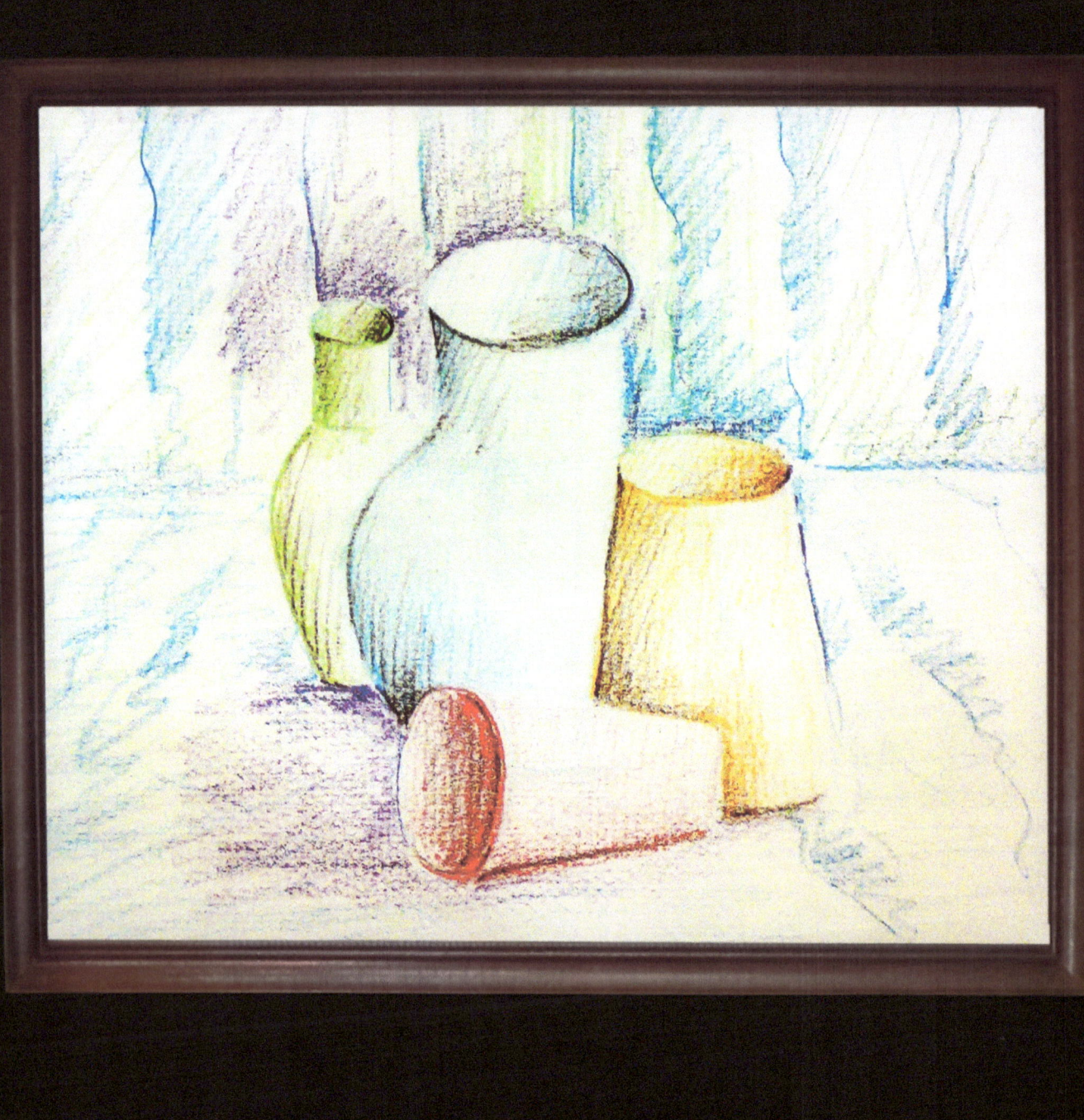

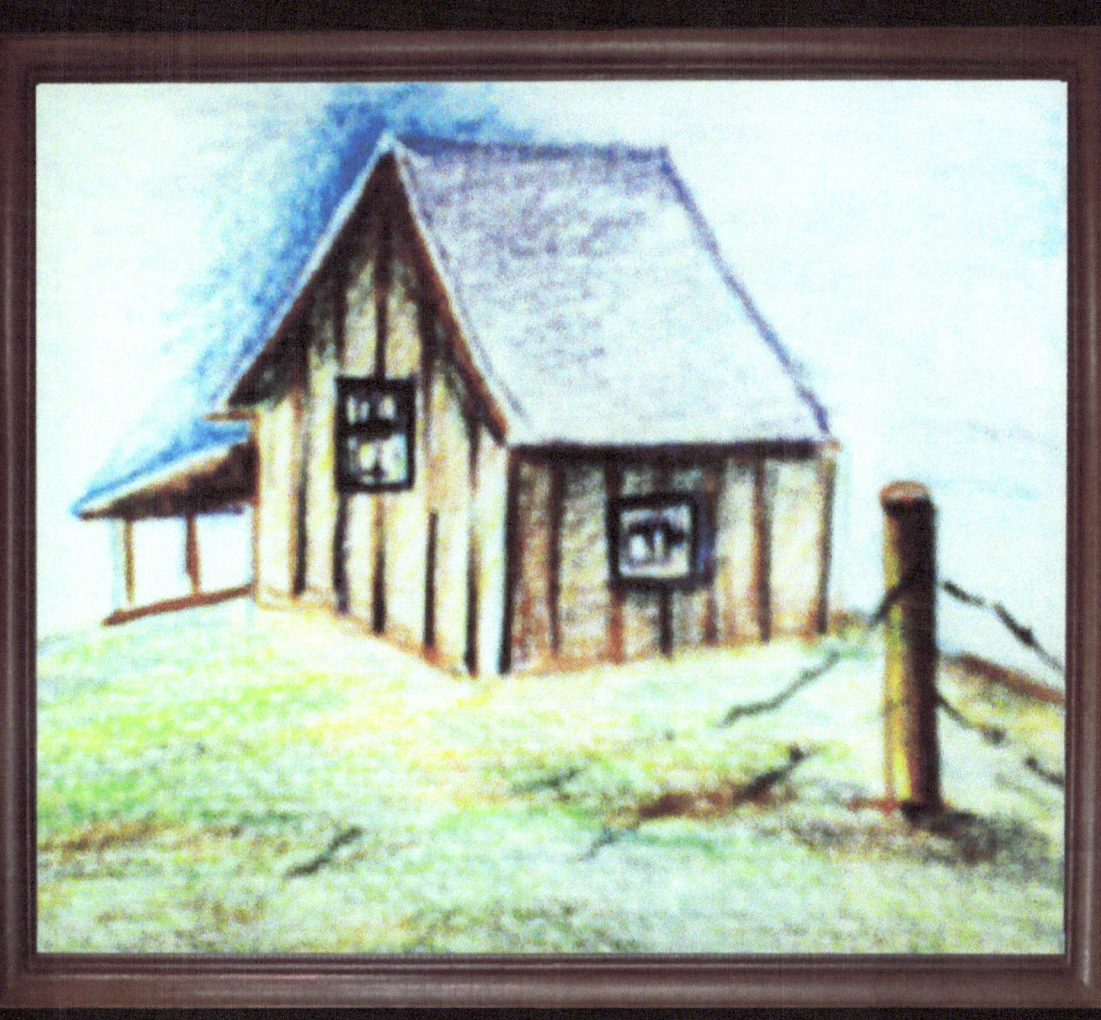

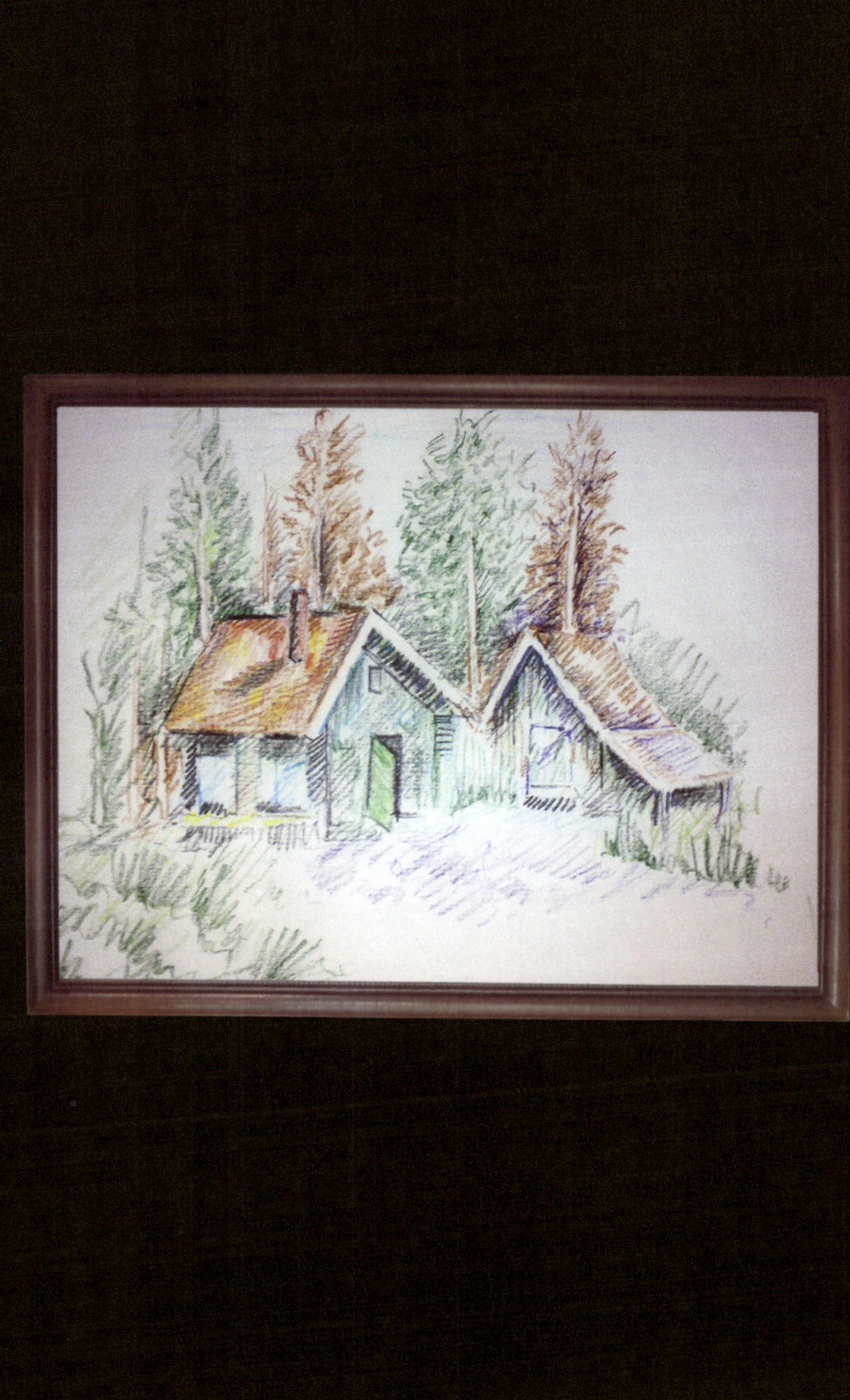

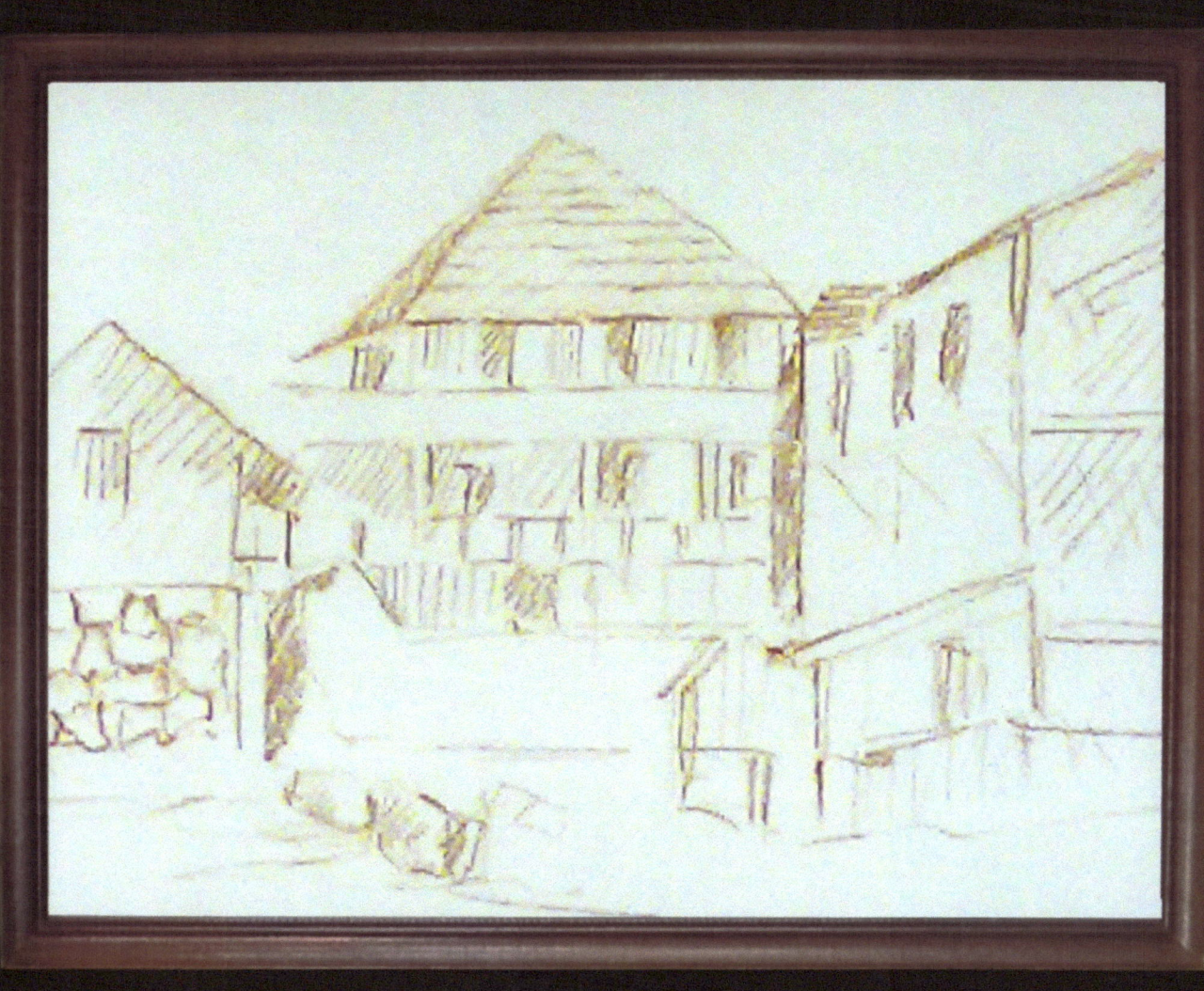

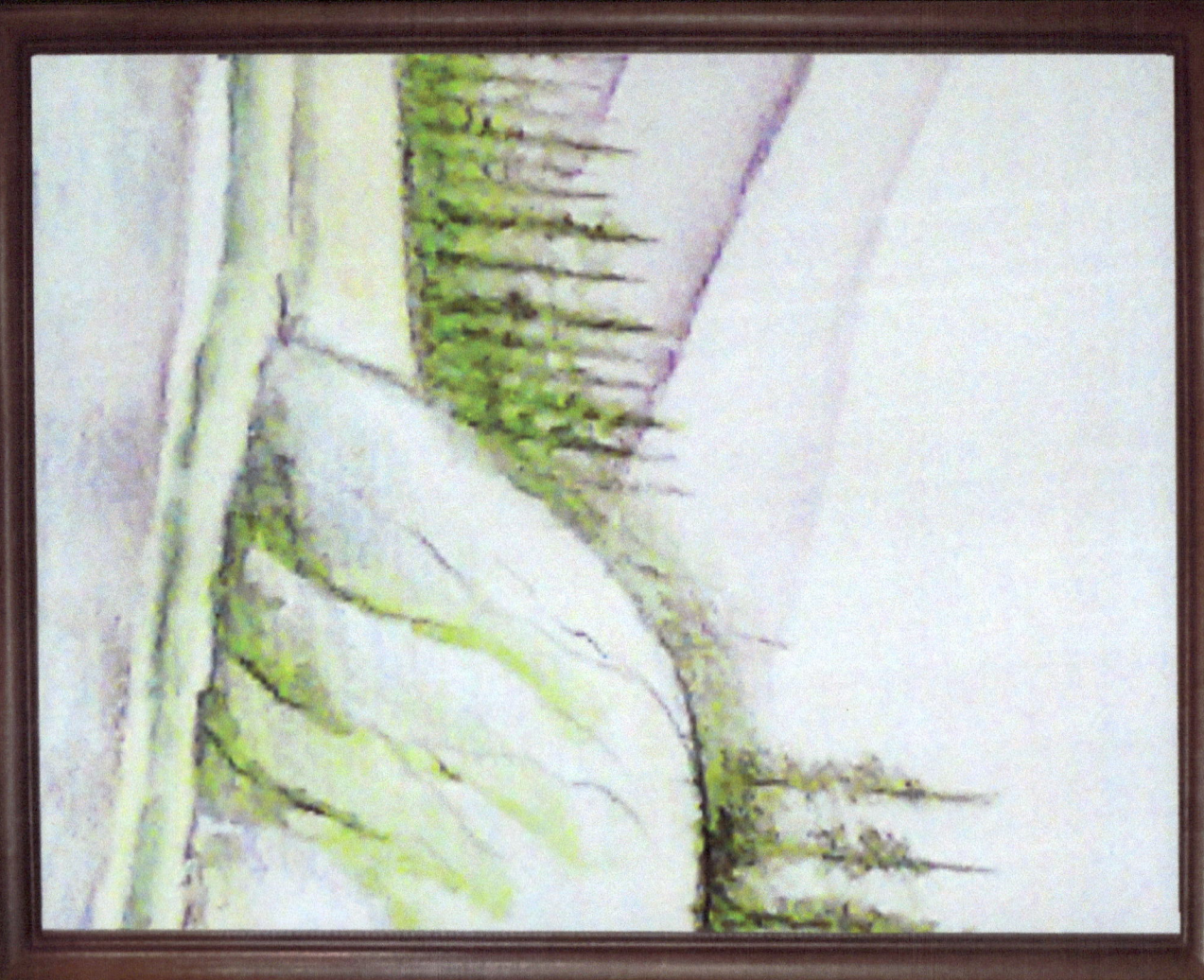

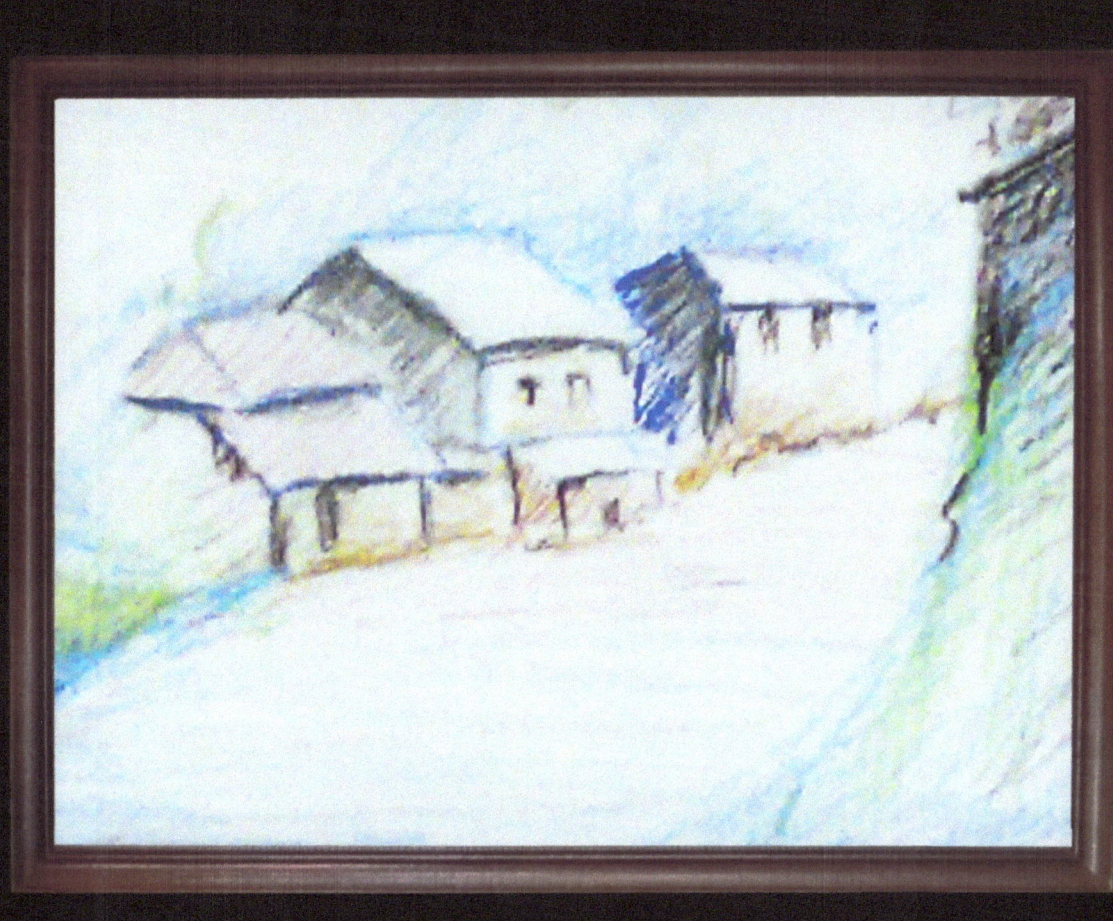

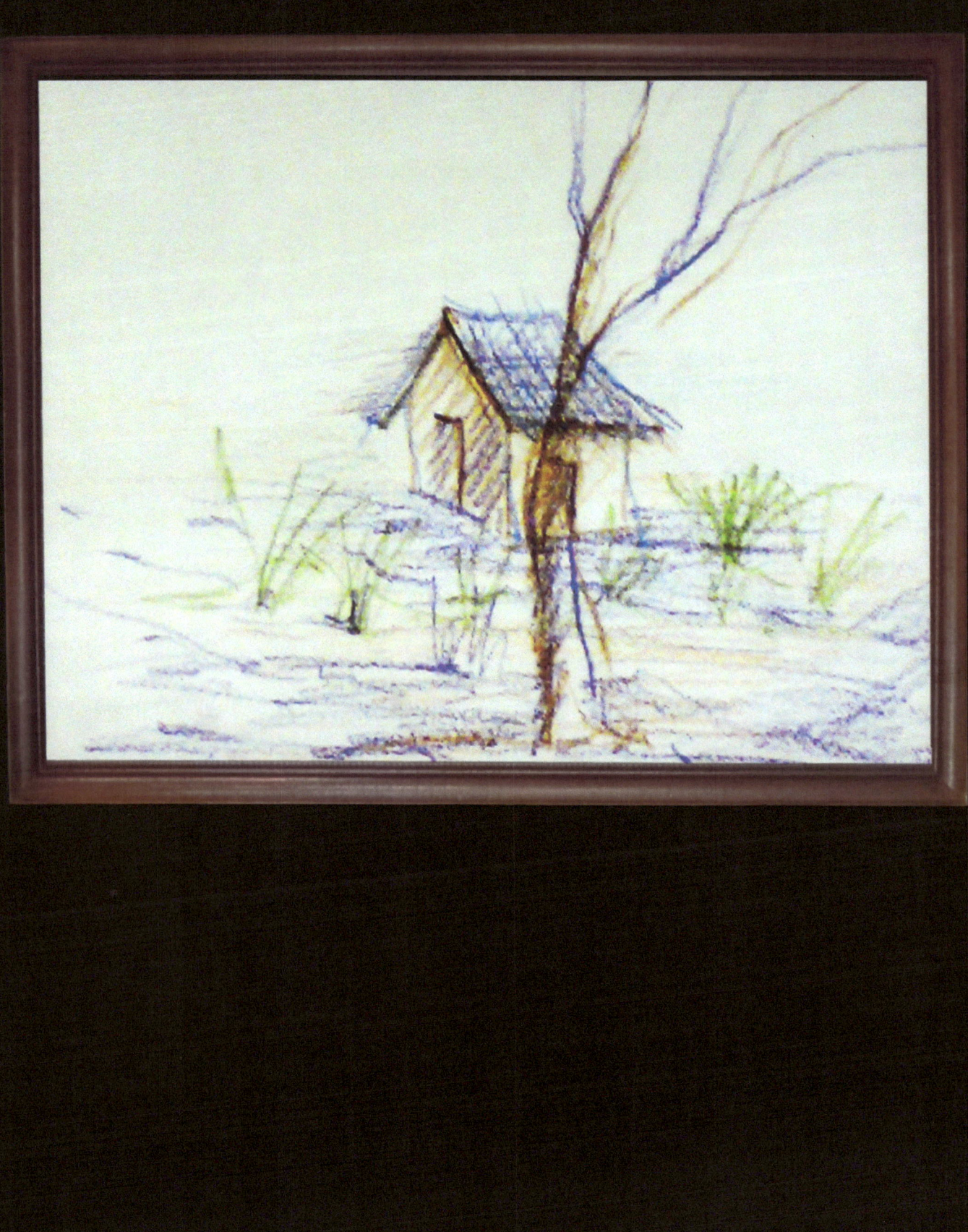

THE END

www.ingramcontent.com/pod-product-compliance
Lightning Source LLC
Chambersburg PA
CBHW050434180526
45159CB00006B/2535